single grape wines

·Ho
to 1

alain simon

→ cabernet
→ merlot
→ zinfandel
→ syrah
→ tempranillo
→ sangiovese
→ chardonnay…

Photographic credits

Corbis *Craig Lovell* 122–123 h. **Scope** *Jean-Luc Barde* 18–19, 22–23 b., 24–25, 26, 34–35 b.,
38–39 b., 40–41, 42–43 h., 44–45, 50–51 h., 54–55 b., 62–63 b., 66–67 h., 77 b., 82–83 b.,
92–93, 94–95 h., 100–101, 106–107 t. and b., 110–111 t. and b., 112–113, 114–115 b., 118–119
h., 124–125, 126–127 – *Bernard Galeron* 90–91 t. – *Michel Gotin* 52–53 – *Philip Gould* 12–13
b., 122–123 b. – *Christian Goupi* 90–91 b. – *Jacques Guillard* 6, 8–9 b., 10–11, 30–31 t. and b.,
32–33, 34–35 h., 36–37, 42–43 b., 46, 48–49, 50–51 b., 58–59 b., 60–61, 62–63 h., 64–65,
66–67 b., 68–69, 72–73, 78–79 h., 80–81, 82–83 h., 84–85, 86–87 t. and b., 88–89, 102–103
t. and b., 104–105, 108–109, 116–117, 118–119 b., 120–121, 127 – *Michel Guillard* 16, 20–21,
54–55 h., 96–97, 98–99 t. and b. – *Francis Jalain* 4–5 – *Sara Matthews* 70–71 t. and b., 76–77,
78–79 b. – *Michel Plassart* 14–15, 56–57, 94–95 b. *DR* 28–29. **ITV** 12–13 t., 58–59 t., 114–115
t. – *Pierre Mackiewicz* 22–23 t., 38–39 t., 74, 126. **Philippe Caron** photos 'eye, nose, mouth'.
Casina Caldera/DR 8–9 t. **Philippe Vaurès Santamaria** cover

© Fitway Publishing, 2004.
Original editions in French, English, Spanish, Italian

Translation by Translate-A-Book, Oxford

Design and creation: GRAPH'M

ISBN: 2-7528-0027-4
Publisher code: T00027

Dépôt légal: 2004 September

Printed in Malaysia by Tien Wah Press

www.fitwaypublishing.com
Fitway Publishing
12, avenue d'Italie – 75627 Paris cedex 13

Contents

Introduction

Very few people knew anything about grape varieties 20 years ago. Wine-lovers felt it a rather obscure subject, best left to the wine-producers – what mattered to most of us was where the wine came from. We talked in terms of Bordeaux or Burgundy, Rioja or Penedès, Colli or Asti, Kaiserstuhl or Palatinate. Those were the wines of 'Old Europe'. With a few exceptions, French wines were actually subjected to regulations prohibiting any mention of the grape variety on the label, while elsewhere such measures were unnecessary, since nobody was bothered about the grapes. That was before the arrival of wines from the so-called 'New World' – a heterogeneous

term covering Latin America, California, Australia, New Zealand and South Africa. 'New World' is a bit of a misnomer, since South African wines were internationally celebrated from the eighteenth century onwards, and in the nineteenth century Australian wine-producers were already experimenting with methods of wine-growing and wine-making that the Europeans had not yet even dreamed of. Wine-drinkers in these countries called the wine by the name of the grape variety, not by the name of the grower or the area it came from.

Then the wine world was turned upside down. The European wine-growers, hounded by new competition,

responded by appending a back-label detailing the grape variety or blend of varieties that went into the wine, while the 'new' producers, for their part, began revealing details about the *terroir*. As time went on, they discovered the advantage of blending wines that complemented each other. The two sides finished by adopting some, or all, of the principles of the other.

This clash of cultures demonstrates that both approaches were partly right. In the same way that the grape variety makes its mark on the wine, so the *terroir* leaves its imprint on the grape variety. This twin influence is further complicated by a third factor – the blending of two, or even three, grape varieties. How, then, do you go about discerning the respective roles of Merlot and Cabernet in a Bordeaux or a Californian Opus One? The answer is relatively easy: if the wine starts off soft and rounded, then develops elegance and finesse, the Merlot is dominant; if the other way round, the Cabernet has the upper hand. Is a Chardonnay fleshy and fruity or floral and mineral? In the first case, it will have been grown on clay, in the second, on chalky soil. The role of the climate is less important, since wine-growers are canny enough to plant only grape varieties suited to the climate prevailing in their vineyards. You will never see Grenache growing in New Zealand, or Riesling planted in the south of Switzerland.

The colour of a wine reveals more about its age than about the grape variety it was made from. White wines may be pale, or an attractive gold colour with green highlights when young, but with time they will turn to the colour of old gold or, in the case of sweet wines, amber. Young red wines have a purplish colour; with time, a brownish tinge develops, becoming almost orange towards the end of its life. That's the way wine is.

Barbera

*This is essentially an Italian grape variety,
which can vary tremendously in quality. It
is difficult to define, since so many areas
and wine-growers have developed their own
version of it. The Italians have taken it with
them on all their migrations, and it is now
considered Italo-American.*

A brief history

The name Barberi or Barbero has
been traced to thirteenth-century
Monferrato, in the centre of Piedmont,
where many grape varieties for
the Italian wine industry originated,
and there is no doubt that this was
what is known today as Barbera.
It is truly a prince among vines,
capable of producing
150 hectolitres per hectare
(around 1,300 gallons per acre),
although more often the yield is
a quarter of this amount. Some
Italian wine-growers who keep
production down to that lower
level produce the best wines in
the whole peninsula. But the
Italians who emigrated to America
took this generous variety with
them because they knew it could
easily satisfy their demands for
a table wine.

Geography

➜ In Piedmont
Barbera has been let down by its province of origin – only half the vineyards there still grow it.

➜ In Puglia
The poor and arid soil of the heel of Italy limits the yield, allowing the grape variety to bring out fuller expression in the wine.

➜ In California
Planted to satisfy the demands of the Italian immigrants, Barbera is used in blending table wines.

Italian immigrants took Barbera to Argentina, Chile and California, where it is used to produce table wines – losing a little of its soul in the process.

Barbera

Tasting

➔ Alba

The top area for Barbera
production. According to the local
wine-producers (naturally) this is
the home of the best vineyards
and some admirably well-
structured wines.

➔ Asti

Here Barbera is made in the
traditional manner that produces
fruity, rounded wines with the
touch of acidity characteristic
of the grape variety.

To the eye
The colour is a brilliant ruby-red.

On the nose
It offers jam made from red fruit – strawberry, raspberry and cherry – with notes of pepper as a secondary aroma.

On the palate
A straightforward but not aggressive first impression. It has moderate depth, marked by red fruit, and ends on a slightly acid note that assures its freshness.

➜ Monferrato

The slopes found in the home of Barbera do not, perhaps, grow the best examples of the grape variety; wines made here are fairly light and mostly acidic.

barbera

Cabernet Franc

This grape is used in many different blends, and is found both in the greatest wines of Saint-Émilion and the pleasant reds from the Loire. In California it is often confused with Merlot.

A brief history

Its place of origin is uncertain because it is grown all over the vast region of southwest France; its date of origin is similarly vague – sometime before the seventeenth century, but at that time it was known as Bouchet. Bouchet, later transmuted into Cabernet Franc, managed to colonise the vineyards of Pomerol and Saint-Émilion (it constitutes 60% of Château Cheval-Blanc), where it has always been blended with Merlot. Cardinal Richelieu was very taken with it, and got Abbé Breton, his steward, to plant it in the vineyards at Chinon, Bourgueil and Saumur. In the nineteenth century it arrived in the north of Italy.

Geography

→ In Bordeaux

On the right bank of the Gironde (Pomerol and Saint-Émilion), it is used in preference to Cabernet Sauvignon to blend with the always-predominant Merlot, while on the left bank (Médoc) the opposite is the case.

→ In the Loire

It has more or less taken over the slopes and is now completely identified with Chinon, Bourgueil and Saumur-Champigny.

→ In Italy

In Friuli and Veneto it is called Bordo and produces light wines for drinking young.

→ In California

Often confused with Merlot, it is generally blended with Cabernet Sauvignon by wine-producers aiming at a Bordeaux-type wine.

Originating in the Bordeaux region, Cabernet Franc migrated to the Loire and then Italy, before going on to conquer first California, then the world.

Cabernet Franc

Tasting

→ Pomerol and Saint-Émilion

Not so strict as its cousin, Cabernet Sauvignon, when blended with Merlot it brings that touch of acidity and structure which gives balance to great wines.

→ Bourgueil and Chinon

In the predominantly chalky local soil it produces very appealing wines with aromas of violet and raspberry. Sometimes a touch of Cabernet Sauvignon is added to give it a more imposing structure.

The terroir has an important influence on this grape variety, causing its aromas to vary significantly from region to region.

To the eye
In young wine the colour is deep garnet-red, developing ruby shades as it ages.

On the nose
In the Loire wines, aromas of raspberry, cherry and violets are clearly evident. Violets are also present in the Cabernet Franc from Bordeaux, but with additional notes of liquorice and green peppers.

On the palate
The attack is soft and develops into fruity aromas with slightly acidic notes. There are no excessive tannins to inhibit the freshness.

→ Simonini di Favionio
At this vineyard in Puglia, heating the grapes produces the firmness this variety sometimes lacks.

→ The Napa Valley and Sonoma
The wines are generally slightly sweetish, with very fruity aromas, often similar to a Merlot.

Cabernet Sauvignon

This is the most refined and aristocratic of all the grape varieties and it achieved its nobility status in the Médoc.

A brief history

Reputation can sometimes be achieved without a long history, or a prestigious lineage. In 1736, this variety was grown at Cadillac, where Abbé Bellet described it as *petit 'vidure'* – a contraction of *vigne dure* (hard vine). It arrived in the Gironde vineyards only at the end of the eighteenth century when Baron de Branne, owner of one of the early Bordeaux *Grands Domaines,* decided to uproot his white grape vines and plant a black variety. He opted for *petit vidure,* by then called Cabernet Sauvignon, with its vigorous and often

generous nature. It can produce as much as 120 hectolitres per hectare (more than 1,000 gallons per acre), but makes the best wine when the yield is restricted to 40 hectolitres per hectare (around 350 gallons per acre), as is generally the case on the large Bordeaux estates.

Geography

→ In the Médoc and Graves

The dominant grape variety here, it is blended with Merlot to tone down its harshness.

→ In Libournais

Grown in a lesser quantity than Merlot, which flourishes better in the clay soil, it adds structure to that predominant variety.

→ In Languedoc and Provence

It was not planted here until the middle of the 1970s, at a time when an attempt was being made to convert the region to medium-quality grape varieties. Two outstanding exceptions were Mas de Daumas Gassac and Domaine de Trévallon, which planted Bordeaux varieties here, far from their normal location.

→ In California

Influenced by the Bordeaux tradition of grape varieties, wine-growers planted 18,000 hectares (45,000 acres) of Cabernet Sauvignon here. Apart from a few estates (Mondavi, notably) which blend their wines in the Bordeaux tradition, there is nothing worth mentioning about these Cabernet Sauvignon wines, except that they lack suppleness in the early years.

→ In Australia

Of the wines made from Cabernet Sauvignon alone, only those grown on the red clay *terroir* of Coonawarra are of any interest.

Cabernet Sauvignon

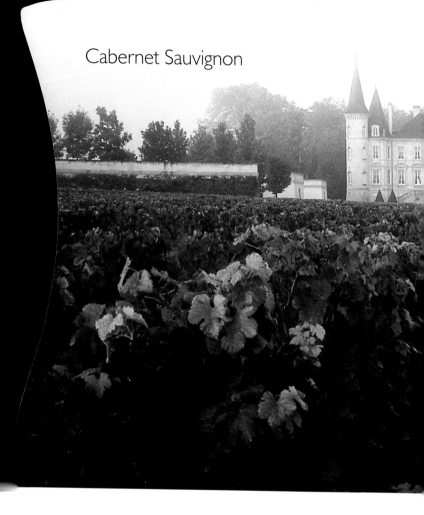

Geography

➜ In Spain

The grape adds rigour to the Tempranillo, the major
component of Vega Sicilia, one of the stars of Ribera del
Duero.

➜ In Italy

From Tuscany, where it was first grown, it spread to Umbria
and is starting to appear in Piedmont, where it could spring a
few surprises on the big wine-producers (Gaja, in particular).

➜ In Chile

With its 11,000 hectares (27,000 acres) of Cabernet Sauvignon, Chile is far from overshadowed by Bordeaux's 33,000 hectares (81,000 acres). The star of the area is Spaniard Miguel Torres Jr., with his Black Label Grand Coronas.

In California alone, the area planted with Cabernet Sauvignon is equal to half the area of the Cabernet vineyards in the Bordeaux region, where it originated.

Cabernet Sauvignon

Tasting

→ The Médoc

With its prestigious commune *appellations* (Margaux, Saint-Julien, Pauillac and Saint-Estèphe), the left bank of the Gironde is the area that best expresses this grape variety, with its infinite variety of nuances, ranging from subtlety (Margaux) to robustness (Saint-Estèphe).

→ Bourgueil

Grown on this *appellation*'s gravelly soil, it is used to give Cabernet Franc the structure and colour it sometimes lacks.

This grape variety, whose rich tannic content makes it quite challenging, has become the established symbol of high quality wines in the vineyards of the world.

To the eye
The young wines are a purplish-black colour, turning to garnet-red with age.

On the nose
It offers notes of cedar, violets and particularly the green peppers characteristic of this variety. Where these dominate, it is an indication that the grapes were still unripe when harvested.

On the palate
The wine can be unpleasant in the early years. The attack is straightforward and develops aromas of black fruit, generally with vanilla or 'toasty' notes caused by its maturation in the cask. Its tannic structure requires several years in the bottle to become rounded.

➜ Sassicaia
With the addition of just a touch of San Giovese, after two years' maturation this wine, produced from vines planted in 1965, develops a silky structure which, in blind tastings, has scored better than the Bordeaux Grands Crus.

Carignan

Praised at one time for its productivity, then cursed and uprooted for the same reason, Carignan is once again in favour.

A brief history

It originated in the vineyards of Cariñena in Aragon, Spain before the twelfth century, at which time it was introduced into France. Its copious production, added to that of Aramon, soon impressed the wine-growers of the Languedoc plain, even though its low alcohol content meant that, during the last century, it had to be mixed with Algerian wine. Judged mediocre, and blamed by the technocrats of agriculture for the excess production of table wines, subsidies were offered to uproot it. But certain producers of fine wines kept some of the very old vines – planted on hillsides, and so less prolific – from which they produce small miracles in bottles.

Geography

→ In Languedoc–Roussillon

This vast wine-growing area is still the best one for Carignan, which is now found mostly in the hills, the lower levels being too productive.

→ In the Rhône valley

Blended with Grenache, with which it was grown in equal quantities, Carignan guaranteed the identity of the *appellation*, but today it is losing ground to Syrah and Mourvèdre.

→ In Spain

Even in Aragon, its birthplace, Carignan has now been overtaken by Grenache, but it is still extensively grown in the Catalan vineyards of Priorato, where it works wonders.

→ In California

Carignan – 'Carignane' to the Americans – is grown in the same quantity as Cabernet Sauvignon. Cultivated for its productivity, the wine it produces is used for blending with others.

Unjustly disparaged in France, this grape variety spread to the vineyards of other parts of Europe before reaching Asian countries.

23

Carignan

Tasting

➜ Saint-Chinian

Planted in schistose soil on the hills of Languedoc, Carignan has a lower yield here and produces wines with black fruit and spice aromas.

➜ Côtes-du-Rhône

Now retreating in the face

When its yield is restricted, Carignan produces wine with an aromatic richness that is unexpected in a variety that is normally blended in wine for everyday consumption.

of Syrah, it still provides the traditional spice and scrubland aromas of the southern Côtes-du-Rhône.

➜ Corbières

Long synonymous with low-extraction wines (meaning that the wine has not been left long enough for desirable phenolics to be extracted from the grape solids during and after fermentation),

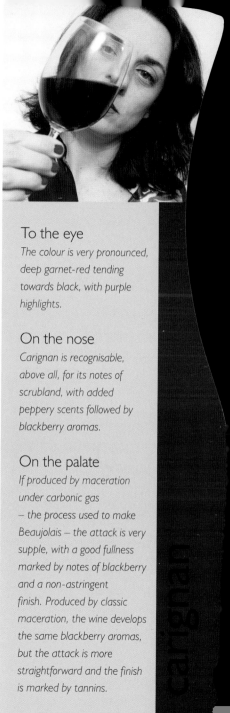

the *appellation* is now more disciplined. Carignan, generally from old vines, brings its notes of scrubland in combination with Grenache.

➜ Priorato

This very sought-after little Catalan vineyard has continued to grow Carignan, planting it in the ideal conditions to restrict its yield and concentrate its aromas.

To the eye
The colour is very pronounced, deep garnet-red tending towards black, with purple highlights.

On the nose
Carignan is recognisable, above all, for its notes of scrubland, with added peppery scents followed by blackberry aromas.

On the palate
If produced by maceration under carbonic gas – the process used to make Beaujolais – the attack is very supple, with a good fullness marked by notes of blackberry and a non-astringent finish. Produced by classic maceration, the wine develops the same blackberry aromas, but the attack is more straightforward and the finish is marked by tannins.

Carignan

Chardonnay

The most widely grown grape variety in the world, even as far afield as Indonesia, Chardonnay is capable of producing the finest-quality wines – Montrachet – as well as the rough wine served in bars.

A brief history

According to the Syrians, Chardonnay originated somewhere between Damascus and the Anti-Lebanon mountain range on the Syria–Lebanon border. It seems that a cunning Crusader took it home as a gift for the monks of the abbey at Cluny or for the Cistercians, who established it in the vineyards of Burgundy, then under their control. Another school of thought maintains that, since it was grown in the same *terroir* as Pinot Noir, it is a white strain that was developed from this variety – a clearly

erroneous theory, as botanists have proved. The fact remains that this most accommodating, most international and most overworked of white varieties is capable of producing both great wines and abominations.

Originally established in the same areas a Noir, Chardonnay itself is indefinable, sinc characteristics are derived from the terro

Geography

➜ In Burgundy

While it is grown in the whole of the Yonne *département*, it is found only in the south of the Côte d'Or and in Saône-et-Loire, especially in the Mâcon *appellation*, where it almost completely predominates.

➜ In the Loire

Here, where it has to compete with other white varieties, it is found principally in the Anjou *appellations*.

➜ In Champagne

It is firmly established in the Côte des Blancs and accounts for one third of the Champagne vineyards.

➜ In Languedoc–Roussillon

Other than in the Limoux *appellation*, it is grown for the production of Vins de Pays or the more ordinary Vins de Cépage. This is, nevertheless, the third largest area of Chardonnay vineyards in France.

➜ In Italy

The vineyards in the northeast (Friuli-Veneto and Trento-Alto Adige) long resisted the advance of Chardonnay, but, since 1983, it has been covered by a *denominazione*.

➜ In Spain

Authorised in Aragón and in Navarra, Chardonnay is restricted for the moment to a few small, isolated areas of these regions, which are dedicated to red wine.

➜ In California

The largest area of Chardonnay vineyards in the world, concentrated in the north of the county of Sonoma and on the most temperate slopes of the Napa valley.

➜ In Oregon

The significant amount of Pinot Noir grown here shows the influence of Burgundy, but wine-growers also grow Chardonnay.

Chardonnay

Tasting

➜ Chablis

The 'purest' form of Chardonnay is that grown on the calcareous and relatively cold slopes of the Chablis region. The best crus have the classic aromas of white flowers, acacia, honey and pears, all sustained by a fine acidity.

➜ Beaune

In this region, which is said to produce the very best white Burgundies, Chardonnay is round and rich. Despite a certain lack of acidity, it is still the basis of the very long-keeping wines such as Puligny and Chassagne-Montrachet.

➜ Champagne

When blended with Pinot Noir, Chardonnay adds floral notes and structure, but the most prestigious Champagnes are made from the unblended Chardonnay blanc de blancs. Grown initially on calcareous soil, in this area it expresses all the purity of its origins; take away the Champagne bubbles and this would be a lean, thoroughbred dry white wine.

To the eye
The colour is a brilliant golden yellow, with green highlights in the young wine.

On the nose
The very complex aromatic strength manifests itself in perfumes of white fruit (peach), exotic fruit (lychees), flowers (acacia and hawthorn). Also present are aromas of fresh butter, brioche and honey.

On the palate
Rounded and rich initially, it deploys the same aromatic complexity found on the bouquet, sustained by a very fine acidity which gives the wine its freshness.

➜ Côtes du Jura
The *terroir* exerts a strong influence on Chardonnay. When subjected to classic wine-making methods it takes on the character of a *vin jaune*, with its walnut and dried fig aromas, and a very evident mineral quality.

➜ Alto Adige
The purity of the Chardonnay grown in the Dolomite valleys is surprising because most of the wine-makers there have stopped maturation in casks.

chardonnay

Chenin

This most anonymous of the grape varieties is also one of the most widespread in the world, found under many different aliases in the various wines in which it is incorporated.

A brief history

Place and date of birth: the abbey at Glanfeuil, Anjou, in 845. The date could be a few years either side but the place is unquestionably correct. Half a century later, it migrated to Mont-Chenin, home of Abbé Cormery, the abbot of Glanfeuil's cousin, which was situated towards Chenonceaux, further up the Loire. That fixed the name of the grape variety and was the start of an international career; the Steen, planted in 27,000 hectares (67,000 acres) of South African vineyards since 1655, is claimed to be Chenin. Add to that 9,000 hectares (22,000 acres) in California and 4,000 (10,000 acres) in Argentina and the world tour is complete. That's how this grape variety came to be the jack of all trades of the wine industry: as a sparkling wine in Limoux, a sweet wine in the Loire and bulk wine in Argentina.

Geography

➜ In the Loire
In this area, where Chenin is most at home, it is made in all its forms: dry, sparkling and sweet.

➜ In South Africa
Despite having imported this variety in the seventeenth century – well ahead of everyone else – South Africa could use it to greater benefit but seems content to continue turning it into rather anonymous sweet wine or table wine.

➜ In California
Here, blended with Sauvignon or Chardonnay to correct its acidity, Chenin loses its identity and above all its keeping qualities.

➜ In Argentina
In the second largest wine-producing area in the world in terms of area planted, Chenin has only had a real presence since wine experts decided it was one of the varieties belonging under the collective name of Pineau Blanc.

First used solely for making sweet Loire wines, the dry white wines now produced from Chenin are appreciated worldwide.

Chenin

Tasting

➜ Vouvray

Whether sparkling or still, dry or *moelleux*, Chenin is identifiable, paradoxically, by a confusing smell of sugar. Rabelais described it as a 'taffeta wine'.

➜ Bonnezeaux and Quart-de-Chaume

Grapes concentrated by noble rot produce wine of an aromatic level undreamed of elsewhere in French wine production. It is supported by an acidity that ensures its freshness.

➜ Blanquette de Limoux

Combined with Mauzac and Chardonnay, Chenin fulfils its role as an acid variety, bringing vitality to a blend wrongly regarded as the 'poor man's Champagne'.

➜ Poverty Bay and Hawkes Bay

New Zealanders, ahead of all the other new wine-producers, understood the value of Chenin when grown in a temperate climate. To both table wines and sweet wines it brings acidity in its finest form – freshness.

To the eye

The colour varies from pale yellow with green highlights, to deep gold in the sweet wines.

On the nose

Floral notes of acacia flowers and linden blossom mingle with lemon, honey and quince perfumes.

On the palate

The initial impression is lively. The development is marked, above all, by aromas of acacia flowers supported by a strong acidic presence in very young wine. The finish is remarkably fresh and open.

→ The Cape Wines

The Cape vineyards were the first in South Africa to plant Chenin. Produced as both 'quaffing' wine and the slightly more pretentious sweet wine, it lacks the conviction of its French or New Zealand cousins.

chenin

Cinsaut

Supremely Mediterranean, Cinsaut has been used for a long time in Languedoc to make good the deficiencies or other grape varieties as a result of over-production.

A brief history

We know little about where and when it came into being, except that it must have been in the southern Rhône valley, around the end of the eighteenth century. It then travelled to Algeria, where its resistance to the sirocco winds, together with its role in improving Carignan and Aramon wines, convinced wine-growers to plant it. Its other great journey was to South Africa, where it was chosen because of its resistance to a hot climate. But for the most part it remains content to play a secondary role. It is re-emerging today in the Languedoc–Roussillon vineyards, together with Mourvèdre and Syrah. It is made into rosé in the Rhône valley and always forms part of the blend for Châteauneuf-du-Pape.

Geography

➜ In the Rhône valley

It makes a minor contribution compared with the other great red varieties, Grenache, Carignan and Syrah.

➜ In Languedoc–Roussillon

Regarded as one of the 'improving' grape varieties, like Syrah and Mourvèdre, it has its place but is used most often in the production of rosés.

➜ In Italy

Renamed Ottavianello, it has found its true place in Puglia and is at its best in a bottle of Ostuni.

➜ In South Africa

Known for many years by the name Hermitage, here as in other locations it is used to blend with grape varieties that are too severe or too high in alcohol.

A grape variety that does best in southern regions, Cinsaut can stand up to drought and high winds. Originating in the Languedoc, it is grown mainly in Morocco and South Africa.

Cinsaut

Tasting

→ Tavel

Together with Grenache, always the major ingredient in this *appellation*, it modifies the alcoholic strength and contributes floral aromas.

→ Coteaux d'Aix

Planted in the hot, arid soil, here the red and white fruit aromas and delicate rose perfume are developed to the full.

Capable of high yields, Cinsaut is generally used to produce rosé wines. Well handled, it can add finesse to Carignan or Grenache.

To the eye
Depending on the chosen method of vinification and the size of yield imposed on the vines, the colour can vary from soft pink to inky black with garnet-red highlights.

On the nose
The initial aromas are of red fruit, combining raspberry and strawberry; the floral secondary aromas (notably roses) mingle with those of dried fruits, hazelnuts and figs.

→ Bellet
Cinsaut plays the role of moderator in the wine from this small, but very famous, *appellation* overlooking Nice.

On the palate
The attack is restrained and the flavours that emerge are marked by red fruit jam. The finish is soft and the tannins scarcely noticeable, even in young wines.

Côt

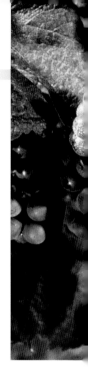

This multifaceted grape variety, which changes its name from region to region and plays both leading and supporting roles, can be found from the Loire to Argentina.

A brief history

Originating in Quercy, more precisely in the vineyards of Cahors, this grape variety has become an unrepentant traveller, adopting identities as varied as they are inexplicable. It may seem logical that it is called Cahors in the Loire, but in Cahors itself it is called Auxerrois. And when a certain Malbeck introduced it to Saint-Émilion and Pomerol, it was given his name but without the final "k". In France it plays a major role only in Cahors, while its true career (as Malbec) took off in Argentina, which grows the largest area of it in the world.

Geography

➜ In the Gironde

Cultivated on the right bank of the Gironde estuary (Saint-Émilion and Pomerol), Côt makes up only an infinitesimal part of the varieties grown, compared with Merlot and Cabernet Franc.

➜ In the Lot

It is strongly represented in the Cahors *appellation*, amounting to 70% of the blend.

➜ In the Loire

The chalky soil softens it and produces a grape that gives fruitiness to the rosés of Anjou and Cheverny.

➜ In Argentina

Strongly represented in the vineyards, particularly in Mendoza, the most 'French' of all the towns in Argentina.

Côt

Tasting

→ Cahors

Here Côt becomes Auxerrois. Blended 70% with Merlot it produces what the English sometimes call 'black wine'. Astringent when young, because of its tannins, it softens with age to take on pleasant blackberry and bilberry aromas.

→ Cabardès

This most Atlantic of the Languedoc–Roussillon vineyards is nevertheless subject to a

Mediterranean influence. Côt is blended with traditional Bordeaux varieties (Merlot and Cabernet) to produce a wine with the finesse of a Médoc combined with the power typical of the wines of the Midi.

→ Touraine

The Côt from both Amboise and Mesland is blended with Cabernet Franc. The chalky soil gives it a certain lightness and concentrates the aromas of red fruit, especially

in the very aromatic but well-structured rosés.

➜ Maipu

Grown at an altitude of 700 metres (2,297 feet), in the Mendoza region of Argentina, Côt is known by its Bordeaux name of Malbec. The wines are black, strong and rich in black fruit aromas.

To the eye
A very pronounced garnet-red colour, with bluish highlights.

On the nose
The aromas of blackberry, bilberry and black cherry are very dominant. There is also a touch of almond.

On the palate
The attack is all-enveloping, giving black fruit aromas and great finesse. The tannins, very evident in the young wine, round out very quickly, leaving notes of black cherry on the finish.

Gamay

Now a synonym for Beaujolais, Gamay is the victim of a form of snobbery that regards it as an 'easy-drinking' wine with no other pretensions. However, it doesn't always conform to this caricature and can develop in surprising ways.

A brief history

Whether the wine-growers of Burgundy like it or not, there is a village called Gamay in the heart of the Côte d'Or. The monks who founded the vineyard, ardent supporters of Pinot Noir, which is capable of producing great wines on its own, obtained an edict from Philip the Bold in 1395, banning cultivation of Gamay vines. This dismayed local wine-growers, who valued this productive variety. It never totally disappeared and, blended at 30% with Pinot, goes into Passe-Tout-Grain. Relegated to southern Burgundy and Beaujolais, it is found in small vineyards that need a fruity grape variety.

Gamay's image has been tainted by its association with the mass sales of Beaujolais nouveau. Looked upon as an 'easy' variety, it is still capable of aromatic complexity.

Geography

→ In Burgundy

Gamay has nearly disappeared from the Côte d'Or *département*, where Pinot Noir monopolises. It still exists in the Côte Chalonnaise.

→ In Beaujolais

Almost all the vineyards are planted with Gamay. The particular characteristics of the *terroirs* of the various areas have created a hierarchy among the nine crus (Juliénas, Brouilly, Morgon etc.) and the simple Beaujolais *appellation*.

→ In the Loire

Most of the Gamay is to be found in the vineyards of Blois and Tours where it is often blended with Cabernet Franc

→ In Switzerland

The vineyards of Vaud, Valais and Geneva now grow it but often blend it with Pinot Noir.

→ In California

The few wines that carry the label 'Gamay' have nothing in common with those of France or Switzerland. They are more closely related to the Valdiguié of southwest France.

43

Gamay

Tasting

➜ Beaujolais

Planted in granitic soil, Gamay produces Burgundy-type wines; grown in calcareous clay soil, the resulting wine is very fruity. Carbonic maceration, mostly used for wines for drinking young, further enhances these aromas.

➜ Savoie

While the fruitiness is still there, notably as strawberry aromas, the mineral element definitely has the upper hand, giving a wine with a more 'aristocratic' character.

➜ Touraine

The chalky or siliceous clay soil gives the wine a marked aroma of cherries.

➜ Dôle

This Swiss wine, sometimes a blend of Pinot Noir with Gamay, is an intimate mix of the fruitiness of the grape variety with the mineral element of the *terroir*.

Gamay is particularly affected by its terroir, and it differs widely, depending on whether it is grown in Switzerland, Savoie or in the Beaujolais region where it originated.

To the eye

In young wines, the colour is ruby-red with purple highlights, turning garnet-red with age.

On the nose

Wherever they come from, all the wines have one thing in common: the initial aroma is of strawberries. Secondary aromas follow: raspberry or fruit drops in young Beaujolais, cherry and violets in Loire wines, chalk and flint in those from Alpine areas.

On the palate

A fresh and clean attack develops into very fruity aromas, echoing the pleasantly acidic bouquet. The tannins are subtle, allowing the fruit to dominate the finish.

gamay

Gewürztraminer

Sometimes a near-caricature of itself, Gewürztraminer's name also reveals its character: gewürz, *in German, means spice. It can easily be identified among a thousand others.*

A brief history

Around the year 1000, the existence is mentioned of vines in the village of Tramin (or Termeno, now in the Italian Tyrol), which, unsurprisingly, were called *Traminer.* They were, in fact, nothing less than a descendant of the Greek variety, *uva aminea,* cultivated in Thessaloníki since the dawn of wine-making. They spread through Europe, via Austria, to the Palatinate in Germany before reaching Alsace. Because of the allure of this grape variety, and because the wine is suitable to drink at any time of day, it was adopted by the New World vineyards, from the USA to South Africa. However, nothing equals the 'late harvest' wines that are a speciality of Germany and Alsace.

Geography

➜ In Alsace

The increased plantation of Gewürztraminer has meant
that Sylvaner has lost out. The wine-drinkers of Alsace
have a strong preference for this spectacular grape variety,
together with the very aristocratic Riesling. Draconian
production conditions make them typical of the wines
produced from the variety, whether dry or late harvest
versions.

➜ In Germany

Apart from the Baden region, where the Alsace-type
wines have a following, the rest of the vineyards produce
nondescript wines, markedly lacking in acidity. In the
Palatinate, the grape is often blended with Riesling.

➜ In Austria

The vineyards of Styria (Steirmark), near Alto-Adige in Italy,
only produce flabby wines, singularly lacking in contrast.

➜ In Italy

Concentrated in the extreme north, in Alto-Adige, the
combined effects of the altitude and the sun could be very
beneficial. Sadly, it is only used here to produce bulk wine.

➜ In California

From any region, and even where it appears to have the
support of the customer, it is a mere caricature of itself:
oily, with fierce aromas.

Gewürztraminer

Tasting

➜ Alsace

Grown in the Grand Cru areas, it manages to seem sweet without leaving any trace of residual sugar. The wines are thoroughbreds, offering citrus fruit aromas mingled with spices. The 'late harvest' wines are absolute perfection.

Its spice aromas make it recognisable among all others, and this grape variety is unanimously acclaimed by wine-lovers. These qualities are particularly evident in its **vendange tardive** *(late harvest) wines.*

➜ Mittelhaardt

This *appellation* in the Palatinate is the centre of development of Gewürztraminer in Alsace. The best German wines of this grape variety, without excess sugars, are produced here.

➜ Kaiserstuhle

In the Baden region, south of Baden-Baden, the slopes of this volcano (the 'Emperor's Seat') are cultivated in terraces divided

To the eye
The colour is golden – old gold with almost pink highlights.

On the nose
At first, citrus fruit (orange, lemon, grapefruit) is very dominant, followed by acacia flowers and honey. The secondary aromas are sweet spices – cinnamon or nutmeg.

On the palate
A straightforward attack, expressed by a pleasant fullness that develops the same aromas as the bouquet. The first impression of sweetness is quickly countered by a touch of acidity that lightens the finish.

between Pinot Noir, Riesling and a Gewürztraminer that is quite similar to that in Alsace, on the opposite bank of the Rhine.

➜ Alto-Adige

The first appearances of the variety were in the vineyards of what is now the Italian Tyrol. The combination of the altitude and the exceptionally sunny climate provide the wine with very exuberant aromas.

gewürztraminer

Grenache

*It would be hard to find a grape
variety more closely identified with hot
regions than Grenache. Rarely used
by itself, it is the basis of most of the
great blended wines of Spain and the
French Midi.*

A brief history

Originally from Aragon, in Spain, it spread to Rioja
before reaching Catalonia, where its name was
changed from *Granaxa* or *Garnacha* to *Lladoner*.
However, the Sardinians dispute this, and accuse
the House of Aragon of stealing it from them.
They call it *cannonau*. Robust, happy in arid and
stony soil, and resistant to violent winds, its natural progression was t
Languedoc, then on to the Rhône valley. Rich in sugar, and therefore
alcohol, and susceptible to oxidation, it forms the basis of the Spanish
rancio wines, and also the natural sweet wines of France.

Geography

Having originated in the Mediterranean basin, Grenache is essential to the wines of the Languedoc, the Rhône valley and Spain. Elsewhere in the world it has experienced only limited success.

➜ In the Rhône valley

It is grown mostly in the southern part of the valley, in the Gard and Vaucluse *départements*, where it is the predominant grape variety.

➜ In Languedoc–Roussillon

Here it has replaced the supposedly mediocre Aramon. Grown on the plain it is too productive and lacks character, although it has a high alcohol content.

➜ In Spain

It makes up a not-inconsiderable part of the Rioja and Navarra wines. It also contributes to those of Catalonia in general and of Priorato in particular.

➜ In Australia

It is grown for table wines in the vineyards of Adelaide and the Clare valley.

➜ In California

Grown in the Central valley and at Mendocino, it is used in the production of quite sweet Clairet.

Grenache

Tasting

➜ Châteauneuf-du-Pape

The shingly local soil is ideal for Grenache, and in this area it is blended with thirteen grape varieties recommended for the *appellation* – a notable exception being Château Rayas, considered one of the greatest Châteauneuf wines, which is 98% Grenache.

➜ Côtes-du-Rhône

Planted on the calcareous-clay slopes of the southern banks of the Rhône, the grape accumulates the sugars that produce its high alcohol content, but the aromas it expresses here are fruity rather than full-bodied.

➜ Banyuls

The poor, shaly soil brings out all the qualities of Grenache and concentrates its sugar content. Put into demijohns and exposed to the climate changes throughout a whole year, the wine takes on the typical aromas of *rancio*.

➜ Rioja

Grown in Rioja Baja, the floor of the valley, with its Mediterranean climate, it is blended with Tempranillo to increase its strength.

Grenache gives of its best when grown in poor, stony soil; the wines it produces when planted in richer, low-lying areas are thin and devoid of character.

To the eye

A garnet-red colour, which on oxidation, or with age, develops brownish nuances.

On the nose

When young, Grenache offers characteristic aromas of cherry and blackberry, with subtle notes of pepper. The scent of dried figs and cocoa develops later.

On the palate

Its expression is generous and all-enveloping, with aromas of cherries in alcohol or of kirsch. Delicate touches of cocoa or coffee appear on the finish, accompanied by a tannic structure that is generally very subtle.

grenache

Merlot

Having become the all-purpose grape variety, easily identifiable in many wines, Merlot tends to be somewhat dull and uninteresting. But this does not prevent it from being the basic ingredient of one of the most highly-rated wines in the world: Château Petrus.

A brief history

The origin of this most famous of the grape varieties is lost in the mists of time. We know that at the end of the eighteenth century it was grown over a large part of the vineyards of Saint-Émilion and Pomerol, which is still the case today. Known as 'Crabutet Noir' before being renamed Merlot (little blackbird), it appeared in the Médoc in the middle of the nineteenth century. Blended with Cabernet Sauvignon, which is known for its austerity and roughness when young, it contributed its own roundness and characteristic fruitiness – reasons why the wine-producers of the New World took to it so readily.

Now the most international of grape varieties because of the rounded quality of the wines produced from it, Merlot is used to make Château Petrus, the most sought-after and expensive wine in the world.

Geography

➜ In the Médoc and Graves
In the minority here, it brings roundness and fruitiness to a blend with Cabernet.

➜ In Pomerol and Saint-Emilion
Grown here as the predominant variety, its tender character is modified by blending with Cabernet Franc and Cabernet Sauvignon.

➜ In Languedoc–Roussillon
Merlot was planted – as was Cabernet Sauvignon – to alleviate the crisis in wine-making created by the mediocre products of the Aramon and Carignan varieties.

➜ In Italy
A productive grape, it usually produces soft, weak wines, except in Umbria and Friuli.

➜ In Washington State
This is the area of America where Merlot is most popular – much more so than in California. Its characteristics and quality vary from one producer to another.

➜ In Australia
Relatively little is grown here, except in the cool areas of the south.

Merlot

Tasting

→ Pomerol

The cold clay of the Pomerol area produces a Merlot of great strength, being aromatic and tannic at the same time. But the tannins, while dense, are silky on the palate. When planted in the sandy areas of Pomerol the same Merlot is much less tannic and is ready for drinking sooner.

With a reputation for 'rich and rounded' qualities, Merlot is greatly influenced by the terroir and can show remarkable finesse, as demonstrated by the wines of Saint-Émilion.

→ Saint-Émilion

Grown in the starfish-bearing limestone of the premier areas of Saint-Émilion, Merlot takes on an excellent tannic strength but its aromas are more subtle than those it derives from clay soils.

→ Languedoc–Roussillon

Marketed under the name of the grape variety or blended in Vin de Pays d'Oc, Merlot appears here just as it is: quite rounded and rich, but without the subtleties conferred on it by the Gironde *terroir.*

→ Umbria and Friuli

It is in these two Italian provinces that Merlot finds the distinction and finesse that compare with a Saint-Émilion.

→ California

Vinified here in the same way as in the Gironde, Californian Merlot combines aromatic richness with a velvety tannic structure more closely resembling a Pomerol than a Saint-Émilion.

To the eye

In the young wine the colour is dense, almost black, with purple highlights, turning to garnet-red tones as it ages.

On the nose

Red fruit jam, blackberry, blackcurrant and prune aromas are underlined by a touch of spice.

On the palate

The attack is very straightforward but well balanced; all the aromas found in the bouquet are developed, together with a pleasant, rich and all-enveloping roundness. This makes it one of the easiest grape varieties to drink young.

merlot

Mondeuse

This grape variety gave its name to a Savoie wine, which, sadly, is only drunk locally and in season. It is seriously underestimated.

A brief history

In his book on agriculture (De re rustica), written a century before the Christian era, Columella, and Pliny after him, mentioned 'the vine of the Allobroges'. The people of the Savoie region of France say they were referring to Mondeuse, but the inhabitants of the Côte-Rôtie claim it was Syrah, while the Italians insist it was Nebbiolo. The first two are probably not far from being right, since Mondeuse is often called Grosse Syrah and DNA analysis of the two varieties shows a clear relationship between them. Confined nowadays to the slopes of Savoie, this grape variety had its glory years before the phylloxera crisis which decimated the French vineyards at the end of the nineteenth century. The influence of Mondeuse at that time extended as far as the vineyards of the Yonne and Nièvre districts.

Geography

➜ In Savoie

In a census of the vineyards, this *département* was found to have the largest area planted with this variety, almost 200 hectares (500 acres), with barely a dozen in Haute-Savoie.

➜ In Ain

With 40 hectares (100 acres), the Ain and Bugey vineyards represent the second largest planted area.

➜ In Australia

A dozen hectares have been planted in the vineyards in the northeast of Victoria state.

➜ In California

Forty or so hectares (around 100 acres) planted in the Napa valley, said to be of the Italian Refosco variety, are in fact Mondeuse.

Closely linked to Savoie, Mondeuse, like the local white grape varieties, has become more widely known through the ever-increasing popularity of winter sports.

Mondeuse

Tasting

➡ Savoie

When planted in the chalky scree of the slopes, this low-yielding grape variety has a concentrated richness that fails to develop when grown on the plains.

➡ Bugey

Mondeuse is found in only very few of the Ain vineyards; it is blended with Poulsard from the Jura, which refines its structure.

Although related to Syrah, Mondeuse has not inherited its intensity of colour. Its wines are clear ruby in colour.

To the eye
The colour is an intense crimson, developing orange highlights as it ages.

On the nose
The aromatic complexity is superb: cherry, strawberry and raspberry, with notes of violets and spices as secondary aromas.

On the palate
The attack is very straightforward, with notes recalling the aromas of the bouquet; it has an underlying body which is well structured.

➜ Chautagne

Mondeuse combines with Gamay and Pinot Noir to give a bouquet of rare complexity.

mondeuse

Mourvèdre

Originally praised, then rejected, and later returned to favour – this ordinary grape variety, Spanish in origin, is typical of Provence and has become established as an 'improving' variety in Languedoc–Roussillon.

A brief history

Grown in Provence for four centuries, the variety originated near towns called Murviedro, one in the Valencia region and the other in Catalonia. Its characteristics – aromatic strength, tannic richness and a guaranteed acidity – have relegated it to the status of a secondary variety, except in wines such as Bandol or Cassis, where it has long been predominant. Abandoned because of its harshness, it returned to favour when 'improving' varieties were required to replace Carignan and Aramon, which were being uprooted.

Geography

➜ In the Rhône valley

From its starting point in the southern Mediterranean, Mourvèdre has spread into part of the southern Rhône valley.

➜ In Languedoc–Roussillon

Considered an 'improving' variety, it compensates – even better than Syrah – for the flabbiness that can affect the predominant grape, Grenache or Carignan.

➜ In Spain

It is the predominant grape variety grown in the eastern vineyards of the peninsula.

➜ In Australia

It is grown on an area of merely 626 hectares (1,546 acres), principally in the Barossa valley.

Rarely used on its own, Mourvèdre is generally blended with Carignan and Grenache to give them structure and richness.

Mourvèdre

Tasting

➡ Bandol

In both red and rosé, the tannic
structure and acidity of this variety
produce wines suitable for laying
down. But rosés for drinking three
or four years on from their vintage
year are a rarity.

➡ Palette

The *appellation* is typified by
Château Simone, the production
of which is barely enough to satisfy
demand: a wine that demands
waiting three or four years for the
pleasure of drinking it.

➜ Minervois

It brings a touch of acidity and tannic structure that might otherwise be lacking in a purely Grenache–Carignan combination.

To the eye

The colour is very vivid – a deep garnet-red with purplish highlights.

On the nose

Wild notes, combining mushrooms and game in the young wine; after a few years in the bottle these give way to black fruit – blackberry and bilberry – enhanced with spices.

On the palate

The attack is clean and generally very full, marked by black fruit and sustained by a strong tannic structure that becomes rounded with maturity.

Muscat Blanc

Wines made from Muscat Blanc, the oldest and most aromatic grape variety, have a somewhat old-fashioned image nowadays. This is a pity – the dry ones can have a very modern taste.

A brief history

There is no point in looking for Muscat's ancestors, since it comes from the very beginning of grapevine genealogy. We do know that it originated in Greece, and was taken partly by invading armies and partly by merchants throughout the Mediterranean. The Romans planted Muscat in the Narbonnaise, the province of ancient Gaul that corresponds to present-day southwest France. It travelled as far as South Africa, where it was made into the legendary sweet wine, Constantia, more popular in the nineteenth century than even the greatest Sauternes.

Geography

➜ In Alsace
Grown on the hills of Alsace since the sixteenth century, Muscat Blanc is now in decline, replaced by the more productive and more robust Muscat Ottonel.

➜ In Languedoc–Roussillon
Muscat is found all over the region in local *appellations* (Frontignan, Lunel, Rivesaltes, Mireval, Saint-Jean-du-Minervois, etc.).

➜ In Italy
In addition to the Asti vineyards in Piedmont, Muscat has taken hold in Lombardy, Sicily and Sardinia.

➜ In Greece
The principal Muscat vineyards are at Patras, on Samos and Cephalonia and some of the other islands.

➜ In California
Plantations of Muscat have tripled in a decade, no doubt because of the momentum given to this grape variety by Robert Modavi.

Muscat Blanc

Tasting

➜ Alsace

Muscat Blanc is often blended with the much poorer-quality Muscat Ottonel. Blended or not, the variety produces fruity, dry wines that are musky but very fresh.

➜ Beaumes-de-Venise

Grown on the Montmirail Dentelles hills in the Vaucluse, Muscat is dedicated here to the production of sweet wines, rich in aromas of citrus and exotic fruits.

➜ Rivesaltes

The vineyards on the plains at the foot of the Pyrenees, facing the Mediterranean, receive intense summer heat. Muscat grapes here produce sweet wines more structured and with more pronounced aromas than anywhere else.

➜ Asti Spumante

Blended with other varieties of grape, Muscat brings its spicy touch to this most famous of Italian sparkling wines.

➜ Moscato di Cagliari

Influenced by the sun and the sea, the sweet wines from the Sardinian vineyards combine aromatic strength and a certain freshness.

➜ Samos

The reputation of wine from the homeland of Muscat is not exaggerated. Wines from Samos are close to perfection, combining smoothness with the finesse produced by a touch of acidity.

➜ Moscato d'Oro

Here the grape variety is not dedicated to the production of sweet wines, and this young, lively, dry Muscat, created by a Californian wine-producer, could become a model for the type.

Known for its marked musky aromas, Muscat was grown by the Romans. It had a brief moment of glory but has subsequently lost a lot of ground.

To the eye
The colour varies from straw-yellow for a dry Muscat to old gold in the sweet version.

On the nose
Aromas of roses followed by a mixture of exotic and dried fruits, with an additional touch of spice (nutmeg or cinnamon) in the sweet wines.

On the palate
The attack is rounded, going on to develop notes of exotic fruit and dried apricots. A touch of acidity gives freshness to the sweet wines, while the dry Muscats finish on a note of bitterness.

muscat blanc

Nebbiolo

A classic of the Italian vineyards and the basis of some very great wines, it is nevertheless often underestimated. However, under certain labels it can command very high prices indeed.

A brief history

The oldest of the grape varieties grown in the Piedmont vineyards – the cradle of Italian wine-production – it suffers unwarranted competition from Cabernet Sauvignon. While the first mention of it dates from 1512, its origins go back at least two centuries before that. Its name derives from the Latin *nebiolium* – the mist that comes up from the plains to the Alba hills at the beginning of autumn. It is known by a variety of names, the best known undoubtedly being Spanna, which is common to Piedmont, Lombardy and the Valle d'Aosta. As a general rule, pure Nebbiolo needs ten years in the cask to soften its tannins.

Geography

→ In Piedmont
Barbaresco takes the lion's share, which is not surprising in Nebbiolo's homeland.

→ In Lombardy
At Brescia, when blended with Cabernet Franc and Barbera, it produces the red Franciacorta, a wine worthy of high praise.

→ In California
The infinitesimal amount grown in the San Joaquin valley is hardly worth mentioning.

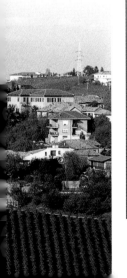

Long restricted to the vineyards of Piedmont, where it produces great wines, Nebbiolo was at one time not widely exported. But now it is established in America, having arrived with Italian immigrants.

Nebbiolo

Tasting

➜ Barbaresco

Varies between elegance and finesse, and hardness and jamminess, depending on the producer. Everything depends on the vinification method used. Gaja produces almost transparent, garnet-red wines, and others use old methods to make wines that are black, tannic and substantial.

➜ Barolo

Here also, the choice is between the worst and the better. The worst is the product of the combined errors of uncontrolled output and being too long in the vat. It is a choice, therefore, between powerful wines with overtones of Madeira and wines of an elegant fruitiness.

To the eye
The colour is a deep, midnight-blue with garnet-red highlights.

On the nose
It offers powerful and very complex aromas, combining black fruit, tar and cedarwood.

On the palate
A straightforward attack precedes powerful development of the same aromas found in the bouquet. Its fullness is impressive; its finish is very tannic and somewhat drying to the mouth in the young wines.

➜ Gattinara
Nebbiolo is blended with Bonarda, which softens it, producing an agreeable wine that has good keeping qualities.

➜ Ghemme
The predominant Nebbiolo is blended with Vespolina in order to subdue it. But the wine needs to be laid down.

Pinot Blanc

Developed from the prestigious Pinot Noir of Burgundy, Pinot Blanc is a variety in search of an identity, ranging from the pleasant Klevner of Alsace to the great Californian Chalone.

A brief history

Where, then, did Pinot Blanc originate? It would seem logical to assume that this offspring of Pinot Noir first appeared in Burgundy. It was known at the end of the nineteenth century in the vine-yards of Côte de Nuits and Chassagne-Montrachet, drowning in a sea of Chardonnay. On the other hand, wine-growers in Alsace claim to have known what they call Klevner since the sixteenth century. But, of course, they tended to give that name to all the varieties of Pinot. Despite its apparent Burgundy origins, it enjoys its greatest success in both Alsace and Germany.

Geography

→ In Alsace

Pinot Blanc is one of the basic Alsatian grape varieties.
Being of only relative nobility, it is a variety to be grown
on the plain, with the hills being reserved for the more
aristocratic Riesling.

→ In Germany

In strong competition with the more banal Müller-Thurgau,
it has successfully invaded the most prestigious area, that of
the vineyards of Baden, on the Swiss and French borders.

→ In Austria

It is well established in Styria and around Lake Neusiedl, as
well as in the Viennese vineyards.

→ In Italy

Its name was implicitly recognised in 1984, when the
distinction was made between it and Chardonnay; it
is principally grown in the vineyards of Friuli and
Venezia Giulia.

→ In California

It found its ideal location in the vineyards of the cooler
Monterey region.

→ In Chile

Here total confusion reigns between Pinot Blanc
and Chardonnay.

→ In Australia

Many of the wines sold under a 'Pinot Blanc' label are
in fact Chardonnay.

Pinot Blanc

Tasting

➜ Alsace

While the Alsace *terroir* gives it a little spicy touch, it is still somewhat inelegant, without marked aromas. Blended with Chasselas and Sylvaner, the common grapes of the plain, it is used to make the unsophisticated quaffing wine, Edelzwicker.

➜ Kaiserstuhl

The slopes of an extinct volcano (literally: 'the Emperor's seat') situated on the other side of the Rhine, facing Alsace, are a Pinot paradise. A little more robust than its Alsatian neighbour, it is also more aromatic.

➜ Rust

Pinot Blanc supplanted the Furminton variety around Austria's Lake Neusiedl. Here the grapes are left to reach the noble rot stage for the production of a sweet wine.

Originating in Burgundy, Pinot Blanc has been very successful – brilliantly so, in fact – in other vineyards in Europe and the rest of the world.

To the eye
The young wine is a pale colour, taking on a golden tone as it ages.

On the nose
Generally not particularly expressive, it reveals aromas of apples and white peaches.

On the palate
A very rounded attack, acquiring fullness on subtle notes of apples and pears, with a strong presence and a medium-length finish.

➜ Collio
In this Friuli wine, Pinot Blanc exhibits a fine liveliness without losing any of its solid structure. It is recognisable by its russet apple aromas.

➜ Chalone
Grown on the slopes of Monterey, Pinot Blanc is treated here in the same way as its noble competitor, Chardonnay: matured in new oak casks, which give it vanilla aromas.

pinot blanc

Pinot Gris

International diplomacy can sometimes determine the names of grape varieties: in Alsace, Tokay (reserved for Hungarian wines) will in 2006 assume the identity Pinot Gris.

A brief history

Pinot *Beurot* – *beurot* meaning 'drab grey', referring to the colour of the habits worn by monks – spread from Burgundy, like all the members of the Pinot Noir family, crossing Germany and finishing up in Hungary. General von Schwendi, who conquered the Turks during the battles of 1568, took it with him to Alsace, where he owned an estate. As a result of negotiations held with the European Union, Hungary has reclaimed the name Tokay, which it considered to have been stolen by Alsace and, to a lesser degree, by the Italians, with their Tokai Friulano.

Geography

➜ In France
Alsace has a near-monopoly of
Pinot Gris, only shared with a tiny
amount of production in the Loire.

➜ Baden
Rülander has been introduced to
the vineyards of southern Germany,
notably the two exceptional *terroirs*
of Kaiserstuhl and Kraichgau.

➜ In Italy
Here, depending on the vineyard,
Pinot Gris ranges from the best to
the mediocre. The best are found
at Trentino, Alto-Adige and Friuli. It
is improving in Emilia-Romagna.

Another grape originating in Burgundy, Pinot Gris
was sometimes known as Tokay – until
the Hungarians claimed back their monopoly
of that denomination – when grown in
the vineyards of Alsace, Germany and Italy.

Pinot Gris

Tasting

→ Alsace

Because of its qualities in the production of late-harvest wines, it was introduced to the slopes of the Grands Crus. Its aromatic expression, though restrained in the dry wines, gains in concentration and complexity in the sweet ones.

→ Kraichgau

The grape – called Rülander here – used in the production of this Baden wine gives it powerful aromas with smoky notes.

To the eye
Golden yellow in the majority of wines, the colour may take on pinkish highlights.

On the nose
Only with age does Pinot Gris acquire its finest aromatic expression, marked by honey, damp woodland, smoky notes and, in the late-harvest wines, aromas of exotic fruit.

On the palate
It develops with pleasing opulence, corrected by a delicate touch of acidity which assures the wine's freshness.

→ Colli Orientali
Here Pinot Gris becomes Pinot Grigio. It produces robust wines, not at all lacking in acidity.

pinot gris

Pinot Noir

Vulnerable and sensitive – that sums up Pinot Noir. It is susceptible to disease, which is a nightmare for wine-growers. It is also a dream variety for those same wine-growers, being one that best expresses the qualities of the terroir where it is grown.

A brief history

While its origin is indeterminate, the history of Pinot Noir is intimately linked with the vineyards of northern France because of its early ripening qualities. So, from the Middle Ages onwards, Burgundy has been its natural home, followed by the Loire, the wine-growing area closest to the royal tables of Paris. Its glory in Europe thus assured, the monks of Cîteaux and Cluny who founded the Burgundy vineyards recognised its commercial value and banned the plantation of anything else in the vineyards under their jurisdiction, resulting in red Burgundies made from a single grape variety.

Geography

→ In Burgundy

This is the preferred home of Pinot Noir. Here it is not blended, except in the Yonne, where it is combined with the limited Cèsar variety in the Irancy *appellation*.

→ In the Loire

The proximity of the royal and aristocratic houses encouraged its plantation in the Sancerre area in particular, with some presence in other regions.

→ In the Jura and Savoy

Here it has acquired the status of main red grape variety alongside the regional varieties of Poulsard and Mondeuse.

→ In Oregon

Pinot Noir has performed wonders in this state's vineyards, which without doubt produce the closest thing to Burgundy in the whole of the United States.

→ In California

The fame of the wines from Burgundy have made it one of the major varieties in the Californian vineyards. The local climatic conditions give it more powerful characteristics than elsewhere, tending more towards plum aromas.

Pinot Noir

Tasting

→ Bourgogne Côte-de-Nuit

The calcareous-clay soil produces powerful, structured wines in the form of Chambertin, Vosne-Romanée or Chambolle-Musigny, with such renowned *climats* (a term used in Burgundy to describe a specific area of a vineyard) as Romanée-Conti or Clos de Vougeot.

Pinot Noir is a delicate grape variety. It fares well in temperate climates, where it gives of its best.

→ Bourgogne Côte-de-Beaune

The calcareous-clay soil gives the wines finesse, fruitiness and an attractive fullness. Two of the most renowned are Pommard and Volnay.

→ Sancerre

The calcareous and siliceous soil of the Sancerre region permits Pinot Noir to express all its fruity aromas, in particular red fruit.

→ Champagne

The white juice of Pinot is not allowed to be coloured by the skins and, together with Chardonnay, forms a part of the blend. While Chardonnay produces characteristic buttery, flowery aromas, Pinot's presence shows as fruitiness.

→ Alsace

Grown on calcareous soil, Pinot Noir is agreeable, fresh, fruity, and of a less intense colour than when grown in Burgundy.

To the eye

The colour of the young wines is brilliant ruby-red, sometimes a little on the light side. The Côte-de-Nuits wines are a more intense colour.

On the nose

Strongly influenced by the terroir, it is marked by fruit aromas combining cherry, strawberry and raspberry. The Californian Pinot Noir gives off the scent of plums. Older wines are marked by notes of game and leather.

On the palate

The attack is supple and develops with an attractive fullness, marked by notes of cherries in alcohol and red fruit. The structure, generally not very tannic, is always silky, with a very fresh finish.

pinot noir

Riesling

The ancestors of Riesling were Roman, but this grape variety has now become clearly identified with Germany. More than any other white variety it has a multifaceted reputation for elegance and distinction.

A brief history

Could this be the *argitis minor* of the Romans, as suggested by the writings of Pliny? Whether or not this is correct, it quickly became the stock variety of Germany and the Rhineland because it was more resistant than others to severe cold. Grown on the banks of the Rhine and the Moselle from the ninth century onwards, it was planted in all the German vineyards together with Müller-Thurgau, a variety developed from it. But it owes its established position to the fact that it was the only grape variety grown in the vineyards of Johannisberg castle, which belonged to the powerful Metternich family. It travelled with the various waves of German migrants before its undoubted qualities became universally recognised. In France, it is strictly confined to Alsace, its cultivation being banned any further than 50 kilometres (30 miles) from the German border.

Geography

→ In Alsace

Over the years, this has become recognised as the other homeland of Riesling, after Germany. In competition with Gewürztraminer (quite different aromatically), the variety has taken over the areas abandoned by Sylvaner, which was regarded as too plebeian.

→ In Germany

Many wine-growers in Riesling's homeland have taken the easy way out by planting a close relative of the variety, Müller-Thurgau, which is infinitely less rich in aromas but easier to grow. Only the Rhine valley, south of Bonn, is worthy of note.

→ In California

Thanks to the local climatic conditions, Sonoma county and the southern part of the Napa valley have made a speciality of Riesling late-harvest wines.

→ In Australia

German immigrants introduced Riesling into the Barossa valley, where its admirable success has encouraged other wine-growers in the southern part of the country to plant it.

Riesling

Tasting

➜ The Lorelei

In this legendary part of the Rhine valley to the south of Koblenz, the characteristic geology of slate shale combined with a warm, damp climate are ideal conditions for the production of remarkable late-harvest wines (Beerenauslese).

➜ Rheingau

The shaly clay slopes of this region (Johannisberg, the revered centre for Riesling, is in the centre of it) produces one of the purest expressions of the variety. Its acidity is moderate but it has mineral qualities and smoky notes.

➜ Ortenau

Immediately to the south of Baden-Baden, on the slopes of the Rhine valley opposite those of Alsace, Riesling takes on mineral accents, sustained by an attractive degree of acidity.

To the eye

The colour is pale gold with some green highlights in the young wine.

On the nose

Real complexity. One can discern the characteristic aromas of hawthorn blossom, lemon, peach, linden flowers and flint. After ten years, the wine releases the aroma of petroleum.

On the palate

Most straightforward in attack, it is very honest, and clearly expresses the aromas found in the bouquet. German Riesling leaves one with less of a sensation of alcohol than the Alsatian variety but, in both, the finish is marked by an impression of residual sugar, even in dry wines.

Alsace

The product of the fifty or so Grands Crus situated on the slopes, Riesling is only put on the market after eighteen months of maturation. The young wines offer lemony notes, evolving into the characteristic aromas of petroleum as they age. The grapes in these vineyards produce the finest late-harvest wines.

Although having notably different characteristics from those of Chardonnay, Riesling possesses an aromatic richness of such intensity that it is also grown and appreciated.

riesling

Sangiovese

*Found all over the Italian peninsula
– the only place it is grown except for
Corsica, where they call it Nelliucciu
– it can form the basis of the most
banal Chianti or the most expensive
Brunello de Montalcino.*

A brief history

Its birthplace is Tuscany, which suggests
that its ancestry must have been familiar
to the Etruscans. It is more problematic
to ascertain when it actually appeared
in its present form. It seems likely that it
existed a very long time ago, judging by
its name, which seems to derive from
the Latin *sanguis jovis* (Jupiter's blood).
But the original grape variety has been
joined over the centuries by a series
of clones, of which four principal ones
produce wines that have absolutely
nothing in common with each other,
even discounting the effects of the
different *terroirs* where they are grown.
Sangiovese, common grandparent of
all these clones, produces wines worth
laying down for 20 years, as well as
products only fit to be distilled into
industrial alcohol.

*Typically Italian, with just a limited presence in
the Corsican vineyards, Sangiovese is made into
the best Chianti or Montalcino wines.*

Geography

➔ In Corsica

Very much in evidence on the slopes of Sciacarellu, it is the basis for most of the island's wines, but it is markedly predominant in the Patrimonio *appellation.*

➔ In Tuscany

Sangiovese originated here and is the basis of the area's best wines, sometimes blended with other varieties; in a blend with Cabernet Sauvignon it produces the widely renowned Tignanello d'Antinori.

➔ In Umbria

This region regards Sangiovese as the almost automatic choice for blending with minority varieties.

➔ In Emilia-Romagna

Wine-growers here have become specialists in wines made from Sangiovese alone, the most famous one being Romagna, which is produced in quantities so large as to raise doubts about its quality.

Sangiovese

Tasting

➜ Chianti

No less than 7,000 wine-producers and an infinite variety of *terroirs* make it impossible to determine a typical Chianti, especially as the regulations governing it allow the addition of a viable proportion of white grapes. Among wines made from Sangiovese alone, the range goes from characterless wines, intended for drinking young, to great, concentrated wines that need to be laid down for several years.

➜ Montalcino

At the end of the nineteenth century, the Biondi-Santi family, a line of wine-makers going back six centuries, planted a Sangiovese clone, Brunello ('little brown'), that came to produce great wines. While there is some inconsistency between the different vineyards, for the most part the wines are fleshy, powerful and initially rather austere.

➜ Montepulciano

This wine has also become identified with Sangiovese, or one of its variants. Generally more

To the eye

According to the vinification method employed, the colour can range from deep ruby-red to garnet-red, sometimes with orange highlights, betraying early oxidation.

On the nose

It develops aromas of black cherry, blackberry, with a touch of Morello cherry and, in certain terroirs, smoky tones.

On the palate

When made for early consumption it is frank and fresh, with emerging cherry notes. In more carefully developed wines (Brunello de Montalcino, for example), the clean attack gradually gives way to pleasant fullness, marked by blackberry jam. When, after a few years, a wine has reached its peak, the resulting tannins are silky.

concentrated, it is recognisable by the aromas of tar mingled with blackberries or black cherries.

➔ Colli Pesari

This wine from Marche, which borders the Adriatic, comes into the category of light wines for drinking young.

➔ Patrimonio

Grown on the Corsican hills, Sangiovese becomes Niellucciu. It is marked by its black fruit aromas, wild notes and a marked tannic presence.

sangiovese

Sauvignon

Fresh, aromatic, easy to grow,
Sauvignon has miraculously toured the
world without relying on the reputation
of the French Grands Vins. It is a
worthy challenger to Chardonnay.

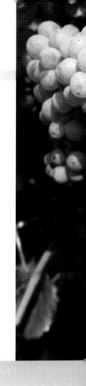

A brief history

It is difficult to ascertain the histories
of the most prolific grape varieties. It
is assumed that Sauvignon originated
in the Gironde, then migrated to
the Loire before embarking on an
international career as legendary as that
of Chardonnay. Worldwide, the latter is
well in the lead, with 165,000 hectares
(more than 400,000 acres)
planted, against Sauvignon's 45,000
(112,000 acres), but both have
become synonymous with white wine.
The use Sauvignon is put to varies
from one French region to another.
In Bordeaux it is only used blended
with Sémillon, to which it gives body,
while the role it plays in the Loire is a
solo one – a vindication for this grape
variety, once tersely described by a
taster as 'the product of a cat peeing
on a gooseberry bush'.

More sensitive than other white varieties to
the conditions of the terroir and climate in
the regions where it is grown, Sauvignon has
an extremely wide aromatic range.

Geography

→ In Aquitaine
Sauvignon, grown less than all the other grapes found in this region, plays a secondary role, especially alongside Sémillon.

→ In the Loire
It has acquired the right to bracket its name – a rare privilege in France – with that of the Touraine *appellation*. It has taken over in the vineyards of Sancerre and Pouilly.

→ In Italy
The best Sauvignon wines come from the Veneto and the slopes of Emilia-Romagna, near Bologna.

→ In California
Sauvignon is fiercely resisted in an area already occupied by Chardonnay.

→ In New Zealand
Of all the antipodean countries, New Zealand has the most suitable climatic conditions and *terroirs* for the production of the best Sauvignon wines.

Sauvignon

Tasting

→ Sauternes

Though making only a very minor contribution (20% in the case of Château d'Yquem), it brings a touch of vitality lacking in the Sémillon it is blended with.

→ Sancerre

Sauvignon plays the solo part here, with an aroma of blackcurrant leaves, augmented by a note of flint borrowed from the local soil.

→ Pouilly-Fumé

The vineyards of Pouilly-sur-Loire are on the other bank of the river, opposite Sancerre. The short distance between the two banks changes the character of the wine. Apart from light mineral notes, here it offers fruitier aromas,

tending towards pear, apple and apricot.

→ Saint-Bris

This is the only place where Sauvignon has strayed into Burgundy, the kingdom of Chardonnay. Although it still retains its characteristic liveliness, the calcareous clay of the Yonne hillsides give it an unequalled roundness.

→ Collio

A model Sauvignon is produced on the chalky hills of the Veneto. Here, Sauvignon wines are as light as they are fruity, combining white peach aromas with those of hawthorn flowers.

➜ The Napa Valley

Robert Mondavi, one of the greatest of the Californian wine-makers, has rehabilitated the local Sauvignon with a period of maturation in cask. Marketed initially as 'Fumé Blanc', it now goes under the label of 'Sauvignon Blanc', and closely resembles Pouilly.

➜ Marlborough

The extraordinarily stony soil of this New Zealand area perfectly suits the Sauvignon vines. Without a doubt the wine produced is one of the best in the world.

To the eye
The colour is pale gold, sometimes almost colourless. Produced in warmer areas it is true gold.

On the nose
It offers the scent of boxwood, aromas of white fruit (apples, peaches) and fine touches of citrus fruit. If harvested too soon, if gives off the aroma of tom-cat urine.

On the palate
The attack is lively, with admirably full apple and peach notes. The finish develops lemony or mineral notes, depending on the conditions in which it is grown.

sauvignon

Sémillon

Its name never appears on the label. Discreet, rarely mentioned by wine writers, Sémillon is nevertheless the basis of the best-known wine in the world – Château d'Yquem.

A brief history

Originating on the borders of the Garonne before confluence with the Dordogne, where it becomes the Gironde, Sémillon leads a much less flamboyant life than the Sauvignon with which it is usually blended. Admittedly it is a little too rounded and is criticised for not being lively enough. This did not stop the South Africans from virtually filling their vineyards with it at the start of the nineteenth century, well before the wine-growers of Chile, Argentina, Australia and California discovered its many virtues. As to the producers in Aquitaine, they have always made the best use of Sémillon's tendency towards flabbiness, using it to produce Sauternes, Loupiac, Cadillac and other sweet Monbazillacs.

Geography

➜ In Aquitaine

Sémillon plays a preponderant role in the vineyards that produce sweet wines (Sauternes and Bergerac). It also constitutes the basis of a blend with Sauvignon.

➜ In Chile

The second largest Sémillon vineyards in the world, producing generally heavy wines.

➜ In California

Grown in climates that are too cold, Sémillon takes on grassy, herbaceous scents; in those that are too hot it is flabby and flat.

➜ In Australia

The Australian wine-producers, headed by James Halliday, found the valleys in New South Wales that were best suited to Sémillon. There they make wines comparing well with the best Burgundies.

While the dry wines made from it tend to be rather dull, Sémillon's qualities really come into their own in the sweet wines, which take on accents of crystallised citrus fruit.

Sémillon

Tasting

➡ Sauternes

The October mists that engulf the Garonne valley to the south of Bordeaux cause botrytis cinerea, a fungus known as 'noble rot', which, in concentrating both the sugars and the aromas in the grapes, gives rise to this sweet wine, with flavours of citrus and dried fruit.

➡ Entre-deux-Mers

Blended with Sauvignon to give it liveliness by adding a touch of

acidity, and with Muscadelle for its spicy notes, Sémillon contributes structure to the wine.

➡ Pessac-Léognan

The only one of the prestigious Bordeaux vineyards to devote a large part of its production to white wines, plays – as with the reds – the blending card. Thus we find a not inconsiderable amount of Sémillon in the rare white Château Haut-Brion.

➜ The Hunter Valley

The hillsides of this valley, along with those of Riverina in New South Wales, produce the best white Sémillon wines anywhere. The climatic conditions are as important as the wine-makers' talent in giving them a freshness and liveliness that is unknown anywhere else.

With its fairly robust structure, Sémillon only gives of its best when botrytis cinerea – the famous 'noble rot' – has concentrated its aromas.

To the eye
A straw-yellow colour in young wines. Very susceptible to oxidation, it takes on amber tones with the years.

On the nose
While not very expressive for a white wine, one can discern aromas of stewed apple, honey and dried fruits. The sweet version offers touches of citrus (predominantly crystallised lemon), pineapple and dried figs.

On the palate
Straightforward in the dry wines, with just notes of stewed apples and a very slight acidity; the sweet wines are rich and unctuous, and extraordinarily aromatic for their type, with a touch of freshness on the finish.

sémillon

Sylvaner

Sylvaner is all too readily made into bulk wine without any consideration for its other possibilities. The best wine-producers of Alsace or Germany can make it into wine that rivals Riesling.

A brief history

Sylvaner has earned itself the reputation of being Austrian in origin – precisely why is not known, since there are barely 60 hectares (150 acres) of it planted there. More probably it came from south of the Carpathians in Transylvania, from where it takes its name. Abandoned today on account of the light, rather acid wines it is reputed to produce, it has made a few comebacks. The best Alsatian wine-growers like it and make it work wonders, in the same way that some of the big producers in Burgundy carry on making wine from Aligoté. Müller-Thurgau, which has invaded the German vineyards, is one of its many offsprings.

Geography

→ In Alsace

Sylvaner may only be cited in
the Haut-Rhin and Bas-Rhin
départements. Victim of a
form of snobbery, it is losing
ground to Pinot Blanc in the
lowland vineyards.

→ In Rheinhessen

Though it is being overtaken in
Germany by Müller-Thurgau,
Sylvaner still represents almost half
the vines planted in the region.

→ In Franconia

While it is still in a minority
compared with the sum of its
rivals, Riesling and Müller-Thurgau,
it is surviving because, in certain
vineyards with calcareous soil,
it produces wines equal to the
great Rieslings.

*Unloved and usually destined for the production
of unpretentious wines for everyday drinking,
Sylvaner is grown only in the vineyards
of Alsace and Germany, some of which turn it
into excellent wines.*

Sylvaner

Tasting

➜ Alsace

Grown in the Bas-Rhin *département*, it has for a long time been the symbol of the region's wines. Certain talented producers turn this acidic wine into a close relative of Riesling, suitable for laying down.

➜ Liebfraumilch

This best known of the German sweet wines is, in most cases, a blend of 70% Sylvaner with other varieties (Riesling, Pinot Gris, etc.) coming from three cantons of Rheinhessen.

To the eye
The colour is pale gold, with some green highlights.

On the nose
Very dominant white flower aromas (hawthorn and acacia), plus the scent of honey balanced with a few lemony touches. Grown in calcareous soil, it can develop a marked mineral character after a few years .

On the palate
The attack is lively. Generally straightforward and very pure, it develops honeyed notes, lightened by the acidity which assures its freshness.

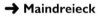

➔ Maindreieck

Translated literally, this wine from Franconia in central Germany, means 'The Main triangle'. The most famous vineyard is Steinwein (stone wine), whose Sylvaner has an extraordinary mineral quality.

sylvaner

Syrah

This is one of the best-known grape varieties in the world – in Australia and California the name has become Shiraz. It has the reputation of being easy to recognise and suits the palates of the New World wine-drinkers: powerful, and vivid in colour.

A brief history

According to a legend born out of its name, it originated in Shiraz, in Iran, and Phocaean merchants brought it to Marseilles, from where it was taken to be planted in the Rhône valley. DNA studies of grape varieties have found it to be related to the Mondeuse of Savoie, a variety that produces larger bunches of grapes. The Romans certainly planted it in the north of the Rhône valley in the third century.

Geography

→ **In the Rhône valley**

The best area for Syrah is in the north of the valley, just south of Lyons, spanning three *départements*, the Rhône, Ardèche and Drôme. It gradually made its way south during the twentieth century.

→ **In the Languedoc–Roussillon**

Because of the consumers' lack of enthusiasm for grape varieties felt to be commonplace, like Aramon and Carignan, the Languedoc wine-growers planted Syrah, which had a reputation as a 'variety improver'. It has a certain aromatic coarseness in these warm latitudes.

→ **In Australia**

Rechristened Shiraz or Hermitage, it is the typical everyday-drinking wine. And unless particular care is taken with the vinification, everyday-drinking wines are all that are produced.

Syrah

Tasting

➜ Côte-Rôtie

Planted on terraces at the very edge of viability for vine cultivation, it has greater finesse when aged for a few years. The strength can be moderated and the complexity adjusted by the addition of 10% Viognier – a white grape variety – during vinification.

Syrah's role is an equivocal one: in the northern Rhône valley it produces some of the greatest wines, whereas in Australia it is made into table wines and elsewhere is used as an 'improving' variety.

➜ Hermitage

Perhaps the most characteristic Syrah is the one grown on the 150 hectares (over 350 acres) of Hermitage. The *terroir* gives it both strength and finesse. At one time these wines were less well thought of, and Hermitage used to be sent to the Gironde to provide a 'tonic' for anaemic Bordeaux wines, adding colour and reinforcing the alcohol level. The Bordeaux wines were then said to have been 'Hermitaged'.

To the eye
The colour is purplish-black in very young wines. Quite susceptible to ageing, it tends to become brownish after about ten years.

On the nose
It is very characteristic, with powerful aromas of violets and blackcurrant, with added secondary aromas of rubber and liquorice.

On the palate
The attack is straightforward and fills the mouth. The aromas found on the nose develop rapidly; the finish is marked by liquorice notes. The tannic structure, generally powerful in young wines, refines with ageing.

→ Cornas and Saint-Joseph

The wines made by these two *appellations*, both from pure Syrah grapes, are more rustic but just as powerful. In both cases, the wine-grower's ability brings out the best in the grape variety's aromatic complexity. They do not, however, have the keeping qualities of Hermitage or Côte-Rôtie.

Tannat

As the name implies, Tannat produces harsh wines that may upset sensitive souls and lovers of smooth, easy-to-drink wines.

A brief history

It is not known exactly when Tannat first appeared, but there is no doubt about where: the rugged green Pyrenean countryside on the borders of Gascony was the birthplace of this grape variety, which produces wines that are powerful, but harsh when young. History records that King Henry IV of France was baptised at Jurançon, and it is certain that red wines from Béarn and Gascony were served at his table. The pilgrims on their way to Santiago de Compostela must surely have taken a supply of wine with them from their last stopping-place before crossing the Pyrenees. The Basques who emigrated to South America, particularly Uruguay, did likewise, but in the form of vines.

Geography

→ In Gascony

Tannat is the trade name of the wines from this region. Though it is tending to lose ground to more convivial varieties, the wines from the *appellations* here could not be made without it.

→ In the Basque country

Tannat remains the basic grape variety grown here, but an increasing proportion of Bordeaux varieties are also grown, as in the Madiran *appellation*.

→ In Uruguay

Imported by Basque immigrants in the nineteenth century, it has colonised the Uruguayan vineyards, and half of the world production of Tannat is now grown here.

Powerful in all its aspects – colour, aroma and tannins – Tannat spread from the vineyards of southwest France with the Basque emigration.

Tannat

Tasting

→ Madiran

Comprising only a restrained 60% of the vines planted in the vineyards (but not of the wines produced), here Tannat is king. The wine needs almost two years in cask before being marketed. Alain Brumont, one of the stars of the *appellation*, offers a Bouscassé Vieilles Vignes and a Montus Prestige made entirely from Tannat. Tamed and rounded as it ages, it develops delicate aromas of raspberry, cherry and toast.

→ Béarn

While they maintain an instinctive attachment to Tannat, the wine-producers of Béarn tone it down to a greater degree than their colleagues in the neighbouring vineyards, blending it in various proportions with Cabernet or Fer Servadou (known here as Pinenc), or even leaving out the Tannat altogether.

→ Irouléguy

The Basque country is another important Tannat area. As at Madiran, it is blended in varying proportions with Cabernet (Franc

and Sauvignon) to soften it. This doesn't stop some wine-growers from producing wines that are 100% Tannat. A rosé version is also produced here. The local *terroir* adds violet and spicy scents to the normal red fruit aromas.

➜ Côtes de Saint-Mont

In this *appellation*, rejuvenated by the efforts of the remarkable cooperative formed by the wine-producers of Plaimont, Tannat holds on to its place, but not as vigorously as in neighbouring Madiran. The resulting wines are more of the Bordeaux type.

To the eye
The colour is an almost black garnet-red with purple highlights.

On the nose
The young wines are marked by powerful aromas of blackberry, bilberry and blackcurrant leaves, evolving with age towards those of raspberry, cherry and toast.

On the palate
The attack is powerful. In a young wine the tannins tend to grab you by the throat. It develops a superb fullness, releasing mingled notes of black and red fruit. With age, the tannins acquire elegance, but still keep the wine's attractive structure.

Tempranillo

Apart from Jerez in the extreme south, there is not a single denominación *in the Iberian Peninsula that doesn't grow some Tempranillo. In every area it expresses the characteristics of the* terroir, *or the particular talents of the wine-maker.*

A brief history

The name itself describes its most important characteristic: deriving from *temprano* (early), it indicates an early-ripening variety. That has nothing to do with its history, of course. Some wine experts maintain that Tempranillo is a hybrid, or at least a derivative, of Burgundy's Pinot Noir and Bordeaux's Cabernet Franc, brought to northern Spain by pilgrims visiting Santiago de Compostela. Such a parentage would appear to make it a compromise between varieties from the two finest French wine-growing areas. It has seduced a few wine-growers in Languedoc–Roussillon, who regarded it as a substitute for Carignan.

Geography

➜ In Languedoc–Roussillon

After a spectacular spurt in the 1980s it dropped back and is now confined to the Hérault, Gard and Aude *départements*.

➜ In Spain

This is the homeland of Tempranillo, and it has several different names. In competition with the French grape varieties, it is resisting all efforts to invade its territory and it resolutely maintains its predominance in Rioja, Catalonia and La Mancha.

➜ In Argentina

With 5,000 hectares (around 12,500 acres), the Argentine vineyards hold second place in world production of Tempranillo.

Other than in the Iberian peninsula, Tempranillo is really only grown in Argentina. Quintessentially Spanish, it produces wines that are fiery and intense.

Tempranillo

Tasting

➜ Navarra

In this *denominación*, the predominant variety, Grenache (Garnacha), is blended with Tempranillo, which tends to assert itself and give more vigour to the wines, with softer aromas than those made from Grenache alone.

➜ Rioja

Generally blended with an equal amount of Grenache, considered to be a little 'flabby' at this latitude, Tempranillo is triumphant in Rioja Alta and Alavesa.

➜ Ribera del Duero

Here Tempranillo is called Tinto Fino (fine red). Blended with the two Bordeaux Cabernets, it is the basis of the legendary Vega Sicilia and the no-less-regarded Pesquera – two wines of finesse and excellent keeping qualities.

➜ Priorato

Planted in the steep Priorato countryside, in Catalonia, it is renamed Ull de Llebre ('hare's eye'). Sometimes blended with Carignan, which gives it a peppery

note, it is the basis of some of the most sought-after wines.

→ Almansa

Tempranillo is called Cencibel in this part of La Mancha. In competition with the Monastrell and Grenache varieties, it is by far the one with the most finesse.

→ Côteaux du Languedoc

For a time here it was considered to be a substitute for the accursed Carignan. It forms part of the blend in Hérault wines, to which it brings a fruity touch.

To the eye
The deep garnet-red colour reveals purplish nuances in the young wines.

On the nose
Very expressive, it mingles red fruit – from cherry to raspberry – and secondary aromas of dried fruit.

On the palate
A very subtle attack, with intense development of flavour, sometimes marked by alcohol but leaving an impression of velvety suppleness.

tempranillo

Viognier

Forty years ago there were only thirty or so hectares (75 acres) of Viognier in the world. Today there are a total of 3,000 hectares (75,000 acres). Viognier became fashionable.

A brief history

There are two versions of its history, both equally plausible. According to one, when the Greeks came up the Rhône they brought the Viognier grape variety, together with Syrah, and planted them on the steep slopes of Côte-Rôtie, Ampuis and Condrieu. The other, later version, maintains that Dalmatian Emperor Probus reinstated the right — abolished by Domitian — to grow vines in Gaul, and planted a grape variety at Condrieu, called Vugava, originally from the island of Vis, off the Dalmatian coast. In either case the variety might well have disappeared had it not been for a few wine 'gurus' who, 20 years ago, became infatuated with the wine and persuaded the world's wine-lovers that this was one of the greatest white grape varieties. They were not so far wrong.

Geography

→ In the northern Rhône valley

Viognier has never strayed outside its historic and natural plantations, which are Condrieu and Château-Grillet, plus Côte-Rôtie, where it complements the Syrah grape.

→ In the southern Rhône valley

It is a component of the blend that makes up Châteauneuf-du-Pape and is blended with Roussanne and Marsanne to make some of the white Côtes-du-Rhône wines.

→ In Languedoc–Roussillon

In accordance with prevailing fashion, the wine industry authorities encouraged the planting of Viognier as part of a plan to produce wines from some fairly unusual grape varieties.

→ In California

Joseph Phelps has reproduced the Côte-Rôtie type of wine production in his Syrah vineyards. A few hectares of Viognier are being planted because it is fashionable!

Viognier

Tasting

➜ Condrieu

The finest expression of the wine-maker's art, both as it is now and as the Greeks, then the Romans, had imagined it. Planted on the steep hillsides, it delivers all its aromatic complexity.

For a long time only grown on the steep slopes of the northern Rhône valley, this white grape variety, with its powerful aromas, has captivated the American consumer.

➜ Château-Grillet

The *appellation* consists solely of the estate of that name, which covers barely 3.7 hectares (9.13 acres) in a rocky amphitheatre near Condrieu. Here they make a Viognier that is so powerful it needs almost two years in the cellar before it can be marketed.

To the eye
The colour is yellow-gold.

On the nose
It has a fine aromatic complexity, mingling honey, acacia flowers, apricot, peach and hawthorn, lightly supported by spices.

On the palate
The attack is rounded, with a fullness on the palate made up of a combination of white and yellow fruit jam, and with a slightly acidic finish.

➜ Côte-Rôtie
Syrah harvested on the Ampuis hillsides is so concentrated at this point that the regulations of the *appellation* allow the addition of 20% Viognier to this grape variety to lighten its structure. The resulting wine has improved aromatic subtlety.

viognier

Zinfandel

This is the most American of all the grape varieties. When ordering a bottle of 'Zin', you could almost forget that it is actually very Italian!

A brief history

In true 'How the West was Won' tradition, this grape variety landed at Long Island at the start of the nineteenth century, made a little detour via Boston then joined a wagon train to California. A nurseryman planted it in 1859 and by the end of the century it was well and truly established in the vineyards. The origin of its American name, Zinfandel, is unknown, but there is no mistaking its roots. It is nothing other than the Italian Primitivo, which flourishes happily on the Adriatic coast, near Bari. Moreover, the wine-producers of that region do not hesitate to label the wines they export across the Atlantic as 'Zinfandel', to the great irritation of the American wine-producers. It is not a *denominazione* but an all-purpose grape variety, which produces red, rosé and white wines, and even late-harvest wines or fortified wine.

Originally from the Adriatic coast of Italy, where it is known as Primitivo, Zinfandel only really came into its own in the United States, where a Californian wine bears its name.

Geography

➜ In California
Zinfandel was planted both on
the northern coast (Creek valley)
and the central coast (Monterey).
It covers about 20,000 hectares
(50,000 acres) in all.

➜ In Italy
The Primitivo vineyards are
concentrated in the south of the
peninsula and especially in the
Puglia region.

Zinfandel

Tasting

➜ Sonoma Zinfandel

A perfectly balanced wine, the product of vines grown in a temperate climate.

➜ Central valley Zinfandel

Under the crushing heat, the grapes only produce wines saturated with sugar, and therefore alcohol, but they are flat and without acidity.

To the eye
A deep, almost black, garnet-red with bluish highlights.

On the nose
The red fruit aromas make the initial impact, followed by floral scents of roses and irises. Some spicy notes develop with age.

On the palate
Very full and marked by alcoholic strength, it offers notes of blackberry and bilberry, sustained by an attractive structure.

➜ Primitivo di Manduria
Rich in alcohol, it is made into a sweet or dry fortified wine, such as port.

➜ Primitivo di Gioia
More balanced, less rich in sugar, it could be the twin of the Sonoma Zinfandel.

The grape varieties of tomorrow

Things go out of fashion, almost disappear for a while, then return to favour. Twenty years ago there was a sudden stampede for sweet wines in general and Sauternes in particular, only to be followed by a collapse in demand that was ruinous for the producers. After that it was the turn of Syrah, then Grenache. And who would have bet that Carignan, less than ten years after it was uprooted in return for subsidies, would be back on the scene again?

How to predict the tastes of tomorrow? Experience shows that the customer progresses from the simple to the subtle; learning to appreciate Merlot leads to the discovery of Cabernet, just as Chardonnay points the way to Riesling. Among the white wines, the indications are that Roussanne and Marsanne (currently invading the

ône valley, Hermitage and Châteauneuf-du-Pape) are following
 trail to stardom blazed by Viognier. And Petit Manseng, presently
wn only in Jurançon, and Vic Bihl's Pacherenc, will no doubt
efit from these wines' return to favour and embark on their own
ernational career.

he case of the reds, Carignan will have its revenge on Syrah
 could soon break out of the Franco–Spanish framework that
fines it at the moment. And hard on its heels is Cabernet Franc,
ch demands to have its say. It is Nature, however, that has
 final word when it comes to wine fashions – once the young
tings have been planted, it takes five years for them to produce
ir first grapes.

Glossary

Acidity: as long as it does not make it smell of vinegar – which would be a major defect – it guarantees freshness in white wines and the ageing process in red wines.

Bitterness: normal in young red wines, but if it persists it denotes that the grapes were insufficiently ripe.

Blend: combination of wines from different grape varieties, as opposed to 'single grape variety wines'.

Botrytis cinerea: also known as 'noble rot', this is a fungus that appears on bunches of grapes, concentrating their sugars and aromas.

Caudalie: unit of sensory measurement of the length of impact a wine has on the palate after swallowing, i.e. how long the aromas persist in the mouth. I caudalie = I second.

Chaptalisation: the addition of sugar to increase alcohol content.

Clavelin: a 60 cl bottle reserved for Jura *vins jaunes*.

Climat: a specific vineyard in an *appellation communale*, i.e. Les Rugiens in Pommard or Les Charmes at Gevrey-Chambertin.

Decanting: pouring wine into a carafe or decanter, avoiding transferring any sediment, to allow the wine to oxygenate. It gives roundness to young wines and revitalises old ones.

Filtration: the straining out of solid particles from the wine. Exaggerated filtration emaciates the wine.

Fining: the addition of a substance such as isinglass in the case of white wines or egg-white for reds, to eliminate any particles in the wine.

Maturation: the process of bringing wine to maturity. It can take place in old or new casks or in vats.

Mutage: arresting the fermentation of the grape by adding alcohol so as to retain the sugars. It is used when making port and Banyuls, among others.

Oxidation: the effect on wine of exposure to oxygen. It takes on brownish tones and loses its liveliness.

Passerillage: concentration by drying grapes on the vine, or on straw. The *vins de paille* from Hermitage and the Jura are made this way.

Sulphur cleansing: the addition of sulphur dioxide to the must at the time of the harvest and when bottling, to control disease.

Tannins: tannins guarantee the structure of the wine. Astringent when young, they become rounded with age.

Terroir: the combination of geological and climatic characteristics.